ONCE UPON A DRAGON

Stranger Safety for Kids (and DRAGONS)

Written by Jean E. Pendziwol

Illustrated by Martine Gourbault

Kids Can Press

One cool autumn day at the end of last week,
My good friend the dragon walked up from the creek.

We wanted to go to the park by the bay,
So I asked Mom and Dad if that was okay.

Mom said, "Great idea!" and grabbing the wagon,
We walked down the street, Mom, me and the dragon.

My friend brought his bear and a storybook, too;
With the swings and the slide we'd have plenty to do.

We swung high on the swings till our feet touched the sun,
Then jumped to the ground and started to run —

A dragon-sized, here-and-there, heart-stopping race,
Up, down and around and all over the place.

Up the ladder we flew, then we hopped on the slide
For a hair-raising, thump-bumping, jumbled-up ride.

Holding on tight, 'round curve and 'round bend,
We were finally tossed in a pile at the end.

I laughed as I picked myself up off the ground,
Then I stopped. Where were we? I looked all around.

The dragon was dressed in a red cloak and hood;
Behind him I spotted a wolf in the wood.

"Oh, Dragon," I said. "Oh, Dragon! Look! Look!
I think that we've landed *INSIDE* of your book!

"Looks like Chapter One," I told my green friend.
"Stay with me and we'll take this path to the book's end."

But that wolf, coming close, said, "It's faster *this* way,"
And pointed to where the deep, dark forest lay.

With his basket, the dragon stepped off of the trail
Like Red Riding Hood does in the storybook tale.

"Stop, Dragon!" I yelled. "That way's lonely and dark;
It's not a safe way to get back to the park.

"Besides, please remember, that wolf is a stranger;
What he says to do could put us in danger."

We followed the path till we reached Chapter Two,
Where a gingerbread house came into view,

Dripping with gumdrops and striped candy canes,
Jelly beans, jujubes and glazed sugar panes.

In the doorway, up licorice steps, calling us in,
Stood a hunchbacked old woman, wrinkled and thin.

"Come in, little dearies," she crooned. "Take a bite,
Fill up your pockets, eat all that you'd like."

Now dragons love candy, I'm sure you all know,
So I grabbed his tail tight and I wouldn't let go.

I dug in my heels as he walked to her stair;
"Dragon," I groaned, "We should NOT go in there!"

With a last longing look, he turned back to me,
And we leaped through the pages into Chapter Three.

Seven pairs of long underwear hung on the line,
And seven small dishes were set out to dine.

And Dragon, dear Dragon, the silliest sight,
Was scrubbing the floor dressed up as Snow White.

I was laughing so hard I missed hearing the knock,
And couldn't stop Dragon, who undid the lock.

Before I could pick myself up off the floor,
That dragon — who shouldn't have — opened the door.

There stood the Queen in an old woman's clothes
Holding out a big apple as red as a rose.

"Dragon!" I hollered with all of my might,
And stopped him before he could take his first bite.

"You don't know it's safe; it could make you quite sick.
Don't fall for that evil Queen's horrible trick."

Then mirror, mirror, on the wall …

Could a gingerbread dragon be fairest of all?

"Run, Dragon, run!" I laughed, "Fast as you can!"
And off through the tale the two of us ran.

We stopped at the river 'cause cookies can't swim —
They get soggy as soon as they start to get in.

A fox offered help; he said, "I'll keep you dry.
Sit here on my back while I swim — don't be shy."

Now I couldn't remember how this story went,
And whether that fox really said what he meant.

So I shook my head "No!" and the dragon did, too,
But the fox kept insisting it's what we should do.

He grinned, licked his lips and said, "Kids, it's okay,
You can't swim across so there's no other way."

My good friend the dragon, he started to go,
He climbed on the fox, but I yelled, "No! NO! **NO!**"

Something about this just didn't feel right,
So I pulled Dragon back with all of my might.

With no time to spare, we escaped Chapter Four,
And joined Prince Charming's guests on the grand ballroom floor.

When the clock chimed at twelve, we knew what to do —
We ran down the steps, where we *both* lost a shoe.

A carriage pulled up and then drove alongside;
"Come on, get in!" called a voice from inside.

"The Three Little Pigs have been captured — it's true!
They need help right away, so they sent for you two."

"You can huff, you can puff," I cried, "We won't get in,
Not by the hair of my chinny-chin-chin."

"Come on, Dragon, run! Let's get away!"
We turned and ran quickly the opposite way.

Through Chapters Six, Seven, Eight and then Nine
(Where we found the Three Pigs who were doing just fine),

We passed Sleeping Beauty, the Little Red Hen,
Tom Thumb and then Goldilocks in Chapter Ten.

I'm not sure how long our adventuring took,
But we finally arrived at the end of the book.

"Now what?" I asked. Feeling puzzled, I frowned.
"We need to find help," I sighed, looking around.

I had no sooner spoken when quick as you please,
A lovely bright light floated down on the breeze —

The blue Fairy Godmother come from afar.
(I could tell it was her by the wand with the star.)

"Dragon! Look there. I think she might know."
So we asked that safe stranger which way we should go.

"I know whom *I'd* ask in a fairy-tale book."
She winked and gave Dragon an all-knowing look.

The End

"Dragon," I cheered, "It's all up to you!"
He nodded his head 'cause he knew what to do.

My fairy-tale friend took a deep breath and then
With one fiery blast blew a hole in "The End."

And there we were piled on the ground by the slide;
"Dragon! We made it! We're back home!" I cried.

My Mom and I hugged and we told her the tale
Of adventure we had on the storybook trail.

Hand in hand, we walked home, Mom, me and my friend,
To live safe ever after. And that is THE END!

The Dragon's Stranger Safety Rhyme

Whatever you do and wherever you go,
Be sure to ask first and let Mom or Dad know.

If ever you're given some food, like a treat,
Have your parents make sure that it's okay to eat.

No matter who asks you to go for a ride,
Stay away from the car and don't get inside.

If you have a feeling that something's not right,
Go quickly to where it is busy and bright.

If you can't get away make a scene — kick and yell.
And when safely back home, make sure that you tell.

Even though most of them won't bring you danger,
Be careful whenever you meet with a stranger.

The dragon now knows some important rules about strangers, and children will pick up many safety tips as they journey through the fairy tales in *Once Upon a Dragon*. As you read the story, talk about the different strangers and what is happening in each situation. Remind your children that strangers are simply people they do not know and that most strangers will not hurt them. Since you can't tell whether strangers are safe or unsafe by how they look, emphasize the importance of *always* practicing safe behavior. Talk to your children about their instinct, the funny feeling that will help them know when something might not be right.

Although the emphasis of this book is stranger safety, it is important to note that most incidents of abuse or abduction involve someone that the child knows. Tell your children it is okay to say "no" to an adult and that they should get away from *any* situation or person that makes them feel uncomfortable. Assure them that if something does happen, it is not their fault and that they should tell you or another trusted adult right away.

Here is a checklist to discuss and put into action together:

- Learn your full name, address and phone number.

- Learn the emergency phone number for your area and post it by the phone. Talk about the times when it might be needed. It doesn't cost any money to dial "0" or "911" from a pay phone.

- If you answer the phone when you are home without an adult, never say you are alone. Tell callers that the person they are asking for is busy and take a message.

- Never answer the door when you are home alone, and don't invite anyone into the house without permission.

- Always get permission before going anywhere. Make sure your parents know whom you will be with, where you will be, the phone number you can be reached at, how you will get there and back and when you will return.

- Never go into anyone's house without asking your parents first.

- Go places with a buddy; it's safer.

- Stay away from dark, lonely places.

- Don't take candy, stickers, tattoos or any other gift from a stranger without asking a parent first.

- Never go with anyone and never get into anyone's car without permission for any reason, even if they ask for help, offer you something special, want to show you something or say your parents sent them. If the person keeps insisting, either run in the opposite direction of the way he or she is driving or go towards someplace busy and bright.

- If someone frightens you, kick, scream, scatter your belongings and make a big scene. Yell "I don't know him!" or "She's not my mother!" As you run away, try to remember as many details about the stranger as you can.

- Police officers, firefighters, lifeguards and teachers are examples of safe strangers. You can ask them for help when someone is bothering you or you are feeling frightened.

- All the rules about strangers also apply to people that you know, even if you know them very well.

- Come up with a silly secret word that only you and your parents know. If your parents need to send someone with a message for you, that person can use the word and you'll know the message is really from your parents.

- Nobody has a right to touch any part of your body, especially parts that would be covered by a bathing suit, or to show you any of their private parts. If someone tries to, tell your parents or another trusted adult right away. If they don't believe you, tell someone else.

- Make sure you tell a trusted adult if you are asked to keep a secret. Some secrets, such as birthday presents, are good, but some secrets may be hiding something that is wrong.

- Most important, listen to your instinct — the funny feeling you get when something doesn't feel right. Get out of the situation and quickly go someplace where it is busy and bright. Tell your parents or another trusted adult, or find a safe stranger to help you.

For Richard, my happily ever after — J.E.P.

To all the Fairy Godmothers who have already lit my path,
and to those I have yet to meet, thank you — M.G.

With thanks to Tara Gauld, Health Promotion Planner, Early Child Development
Injury and Family Abuse Prevention Program, Thunder Bay District Health Unit;
Constable Sean Mulligan, McKellar Neighbourhood Policing, City of Thunder Bay Police;
and Police Constable Tanya Calvert, Community Services Officer, St. Thomas Police Service.

Text © 2006 Jean E. Pendziwol
Illustrations © 2006 Martine Gourbault

Kids Can Press acknowledges the financial support of the Government of Ontario, through the Ontario
Media Development Corporation's Ontario Book Initiative; the Ontario Arts Council; the Canada Council
for the Arts; and the Government of Canada, through the BPIDP, for our publishing activity.

Published in Canada by
Kids Can Press Ltd.
29 Birch Avenue
Toronto, ON M4V 1E2

Published in the U.S. by
Kids Can Press Ltd.
2250 Military Road
Tonawanda, NY 14150

www.kidscanpress.com

The artwork in this book was rendered in pencil crayon.
The text is set in Berkeley.

Edited by Debbie Rogosin
Designed by Karen Powers
Printed and bound in China

The hardcover edition of this book is smyth sewn casebound.
The paperback edition of this book is limp sewn with a drawn-on cover.

CM 06   0 9 8 7 6 5 4 3 2
CM PA 06   0 9 8 7 6 5 4 3 2

Library and Archives Canada Cataloguing in Publication

Pendziwol, Jean
     Once upon a dragon : stranger safety for kids (and dragons) / written by Jean E. Pendziwol ;
illustrated by Martine Gourbault.

Ages: 3–7
ISBN 978-1-55337-722-1 (bound).
ISBN 978-1-55337-969-0 (pbk.).

1. Children and strangers — Juvenile fiction. 2. Children — Crimes
against — Prevention — Juvenile fiction. 3. Picture books for children.
I. Gourbault, Martine II. Title.

PS8581.E55312O53 2006   jC813'.54   C2005-903652-4

Kids Can Press is a  Entertainment company